#Real Estate and Chill

by

P. E. Barnes

DEDICATION

This book is dedicated to my children, Benjamin and Franklin, my constant source of joy and inspiration. I can't wait to pass the baton to these two future investors. An extra special thanks to my husband, my best friend, and my business partner; I love you for all the encouragement and support. We are an amazing team. I can't imagine spending my weekends in the hardware store with anyone else but you...LOL. My mother, who is always there to uplift and offer words of wisdom. Thanks for the unconditional love and support, for you are an intricate part of our success.

PREFACE

In 2005, during the real-estate bubble, my husband and I purchased our first property; a condo, with no money down. During this time there were only a few bank requirements to purchase real estate. A pulse and the ability to sign a document. I was 20 years old and a college student. I sold that property one year later and had to bring $1100 to the closing table to sell that property. I was pretty devastated, for I thought I would make a tidy profit on the property after putting about 5k in renovations into it.

Homeowners association fees and special assessments absorbed all of our profit. That did not deter me, because that same year my husband and I purchased a second condo in the same building. It was a foreclosure and, after completing some renovations, we listed the condo. It sold after six months, and we walked away with a $13k profit. We took that profit and have been rinsing and repeating with a combination of rentals and flips. Listen, I've taken a few "L"s (losses) as a real estate investor. I want to share some of the lessons and shortcuts from my success along this ongoing journey to financial freedom. I love the independence and lifestyle; it has afforded my family and me. Real-estate investing can foster entrepreneurship, passive income, and allow you to leave an inheritance for your children. This is an opportunity to change your family tree, as Dave Ramsey would say. Real-estate investing is a great career path, and economy proof. I don't claim to have all the answers or one-size-fits all template for success, but I hope this will inspire anyone sitting on the sidelines contemplating investing in real-estate. "Believe you can and you're halfway there."- Theodore Roosevelt.

TABLE OF CONTENTS

Chapter 1

INVESTOR SEEKING AN INVESTOR-FRIENDLY AGENT

BUYING-The first order of business is finding a real estate agent to work with who is compatible with your level of experience and financial goals.

REALTORS

A good real estate agent that specializes in working with investors is an important ingredient for success in real estate investing. Find an agent that specializes in the area of your interest and who enjoys working with investors. This is important because they will be able to identify the good deals. Not every real estate agent desires to work with investors. Investors submit many offers on several different properties, sometimes daily. Typically they request frequent showings for different properties. The last thing you want is a realtor who just wants to close the deal because of apparent fatigue. Realtors who are investors themselves have a better grasp of building a real estate portfolio.

During your quest to find a real estate agent ask friends and family if they have any recommendations. Real estate listing websites also have recommended real estate agents for your area, and they usually accompany a professional description of the agent. Once you have compiled a lists of recommendations make time to call and inquire if they are accepting new clients, ask about their areas of expertise. And most importantly talk to them about your needs and goals.

Moreover, it is not uncommon for real estate investors to work with more than one real estate agent to find deals. Sometimes you need agents that specialize in different areas; maybe you have a realtor for the south-side of town and one for the north-side of town or an agent that specializes in commercial and another for residential. Most realtors work really hard to earn your business and help you achieve your real estate goals. Hence, it is important to be upfront about your financial position, do not waste their time. If you do not have a pre-approval letter or maybe you don't qualify because of some credit issues, be honest and they may be able to refer you to a credit repair company or a bank to get you pre-approved.

It is imperative to cultivate a working relationship with a real estate agent and also network with some of the real estate agents in the area of your interests. Real estate agents will start your search in the MLS (Multiple Listing Service). The, MLS is a major database of home listings, and the most popular outlet buyers search to buy a property. Some real estate agents may have pocket listings, a property for sale, where a broker has a listing agreement with the seller but it is not advertised or entered into the MLS. These deals can be very lucrative. Real estate agents can also keep you informed of any upcoming listings that may be of interests to you.

 The homes on the MLS are represented by real estate agents/brokers, who represent the property for the seller. Some of the popular websites to search properties on the MLS: are www.Realtor.com,www.Zillow.com, www.Redfin.com, etc. When visiting these websites, you can sign up for email alerts for properties in your area of interests. These alerts will notify you of new properties, price reductions, and when properties are no longer available or under contract. Your real estate agent can also sign you up for email alerts within the MLS website.

Chapter 2

THERE ARE SEVERAL WAYS TO

SKIN A CAT.

When you're in the process of looking for your first or fifti-eth property purchase, don't limit yourself to just a real es-tate agent. Let the network of people around you know you are looking to buy. There are many deals out there that are not on the MLS or online. Even family members may know of a neighbor or a friend that desires to sell. If you have a particular neighborhood that you want to make a purchase in, take some time to drive through the neighborhood and look for "For Sale by Owner" signs, or signs that foretell distressed houses; such as unkept grass, newspapers or mail piled on the porch. These type of properties can be great deals. For Sale by Owner (FSBO) is the selling of real estate without the representation of real estate broker or agent. FSBO may allow you to be more creative with financing, for instance, the owner may offer owner financing or even a better selling price since the seller will not have to pay a selling commission. FSBO transactions have no real estate agents involved; you deal directly with the seller.

If you're searching for FSBO properties, these can be found on Craigslist, the local newspaper, and www.Zillow.com — among a few other websites. All of which allows sellers to list their property for sale without the representation of a real estate agent. Another reason you should sign up for alerts is that the listings that your real estate agent sends will only include properties on the Multiple Listing Service (MLS) or those listed by other agents. Websites like Zillow, Redfin, Trulia, etc. will have FSBO properties available.

Additionally, banks, especially small banks, can be a great resource for buying and financing a property. Sometimes banks have a list of foreclosed properties they want to liquidate; therefore, depending on your credit and capital, this can be a really great option.

An auction site is another alternative. Recently, real-estate auction websites have begun offering financing on some of their inventory, which makes this a viable option. Note that sometimes the auction site allows showings but other times you may have to bid sight unseen, which poses a set of risks. Another disadvantage of real estate auctions are the closing cost fees are higher (ranging from 2-5%) than a traditional property purchase. Ensure you're accounting for that when bidding on the property. Still, some sites require a $2500 deposit to bid while others don't require a deposit.

If you do not win the auction, then the deposit is released back to your credit card/bank account.

My favorite auction website is: Hudson & Marshall www.hudsonandmarshall.com. It requires no deposit, and the process is seamless. Others that I frequent are www.hubzu.com, www.auction.com, www.homesearch.com If you do a quick Google search, there are many others. Research, research, research the property you're bidding on, for I cannot emphasize this enough. Some of these properties have liens, or building code violations, or really expensive repairs. Be informed and seek the advice of your real estate agent and attorney. The great thing about auctions is your real estate agent can receive a commission from your purchase.

Most auction websites have a disclaimer on their websites that informs you of their rights to engage in shill bidding on behalf of the seller. This means the auctioneer may open the auction on a property by placing that first bid and placing consecutive bids on the property to compete with other bidders to increase the selling price of the property. Keep this in mind when you are bidding to prevent overpaying, the goal is to be in an equitable position. There are also courthouse auctions. Typically, foreclosure auctions take place at the county courthouse, a sheriff or trustee conducts the auction.

Furthermore, Housing and Urban Development (HUD) homes are foreclosed homes ranging from one to four units acquired by the Department of Housing and Urban Development. However, they usually allow a 10-day bidding period for first-time homebuyers or owner-occupied bidders; then they allow investors to bid after that period has expired. I have successfully purchased a couple of properties with HUD. There is a considerable amount of paperwork involved and the deadlines are strict. Ensure your agent is familiar with HUD guidelines and is also registered with the website. Agent registration is required for you to bid on the website. Additionally, in my experience, HUD, does not pay the traditional sellers closing costs. They pass those costs along to the buyer, thereby increasing your closings

costs.

Chapter 3

THE HOOD, AND THE GOOD

Neighborhoods:

Low Income

Low-income neighborhoods can be a great place to start if you are new to real estate investing and you don't qualify for a loan or only qualify for a small loan. These neighborhoods offer lower valued real estate and typically lower property taxes, but that is not a given. Some low-income neighborhoods have property taxes in the tens of thousands annually, so always check and verify taxes before buying. These properties are generally heavy on cash flow and low on appreciation. Cash flow is the proceeds from rent after mortgage payments, capital expenditures, utilities, property taxes, maintenance, insurance expenses and property management are paid. In big cities Section 8 usually pays more than the market rent rate for these homes.

However, keep in mind that low-income tenants generally require a micromanagement approach. Therefore, you spend more of your time handling service requests or complaints. Also, if you're strongly considering investing in a low-income area, you should drive through the neighborhood; sometimes you can find quiet blocks with less crime that are occupied by older homeowners that take care of their property. Visit at night time as well to observe any noise violations, loitering, or crimes. Purchasing in these neighborhoods in the winter months can be a challenge if you live in a colder climate because you don't get an accurate picture of the activity occurring on the block in the warmer months.

Once you decide to invest in lower-income neighborhoods, DON'T BE A SLUMLORD. Having a purpose in this business will give you a passion to go the distance and prosper. Demonstrate pride in your property; clean up and beautify the outside as you do the inside. Respect the tenants; don't cut corners on repairs or updates just because it is a Section 8 tenant or because of the neighborhood. If you cut too many corners in the rehab process and the result is sloppy workmanship, you will attract the worst quality tenants. Good quality tenants will not want to live there; they will have other options.

Another disadvantage, when investing in these neighborhoods is, sometimes finding a property manager for those properties can be difficult. Some property managers are afraid of war zones or crime-ridden neighborhoods. So, you may find yourself with limited options when it comes to managing in low-income areas.

Section 8

Section 8 is formally known as the Housing Choice Voucher Program. It is a federal government program that assists the poor, elderly and disabled with rental housing assistance in the form of a voucher. Typically, when you are buying in low-income areas, Section 8 is a lucrative option for those landlords that are willing to submit to the scrutiny of inspections and strict guidelines. Section 8 has strict housing standards which you must conform to if you want to participate in the program. Some landlords balk at the requirements because depending on the condition of the property, the lists of repairs or requirements can range from 1-20 pages long. After you pass the initial inspection, you are subjected to annual inspections. However, some cities reward landlords that pass inspection on the first attempt the privilege of inspections every two years.

In larger metropolitan cities, Section 8 might pay more than market rent. Thus, it can be worth it financially to submit to pesky inspections. HUD pays you a portion of the rent, and the tenant pays a portion based on their income. Contrary to public opinion, most Section 8 voucher holders are employed, although some are underemployed. However, there are some cases where the tenant pays no portion, and you receive the full amount of rent from HUD. In most cases, this is due to unemployment or physical disability.

CAVEAT: The rent portion of a Section 8 tenant can vary during the lease term, because if there is a change in the tenant's income it will be adjusted. Example: the tenant suffered a job loss. HUD will reduce or eliminate the rent portion and you will receive all or a larger rent portion from HUD. However, if the tenant receives a raise on his/her job, then their rent portion may increase and there will be a decrease in the rent portion of which you receive from HUD. The monthly rent amount will not change.

There are also times when Section 8 will lowball the land-lord and offer less than market rent. Examine other similar units to get an accurate figure for the amount of rent you should receive for your unit. The website: www.socialserve.com can be a great point of reference as well as another marketing tool to advertise your Section 8 property. Section 8 also offers property tax incentives to landlords that rent to tenants in "opportunity areas," these areas are defined as middle to upper class neighborhoods. The local housing agency website will generally have a map of the areas that are eligible for property tax breaks, just type in the property address. Another aspect to consider is the age of the property. Section 8 requirements become even stringent for landlords that have properties that are built prior to 1978, with children under the age of six, be-cause lead paint is a MAJOR concern.

The inspector will spend more time scrutinizing the interior and exterior of the property looking for loose, chipped, and deteriorated paint. Be prepared to paint the house from top to bottom, no kidding. I have discovered places in my properties that I didn't know existed, that required painting. Attics, basement walls, pipes, upper roof siding, fences; you name it, I painted it. The inspections for children under the age of six can be excruciating, but be patient with the inspector. They do not want a child to be exposed to lead paint on their watch, for they could lose their job. The effects of lead poising are irreversible in children.

Management wise, these tenants require a micromanagement approach; you will encounter more service calls and frivolous requests. I personally like to rent to Section 8 tenants new to the program; they are easier to please and don't have the entitlement that some of the veteran voucher holders possess.

On the other hand, some section 8 tenants can have very high expectations on the government's dime. Thus, if you want to attract the better quality voucher holders, finding middle ground on the renovations is imperative. The things that have worked for me are laminate flooring that has the look of hardwoods but very durable for tenants and less expensive than hardwoods. In the kitchen, if you are replacing appliances, select black appliances, they look great and are less expensive than stainless steel appliances. Choose a laminate countertop that has a pattern it will camouflage stains.

Middle and Upper Class

These neighborhoods offer more stable tenants with careers, savings, higher credit scores, and they generally take better care of the property. Additionally, they have fewer service requests. The management required for this class of tenants is more laissez faire, a hands-off approach. These tenants are usually working professionals; they typically don't spend their time making frivolous complaints to management. However, investment properties in these neighborhoods are more expensive to acquire and are typically purchased with loans, they don't generally have great cash flow, but they may have good appreciation. Appreciation is the increase in the value of the property over time.

Example: If you purchased a property for $100,000 and five years later the property is worth $125,000, the property appreciated by 25% over five years. Some investors prefer this route over a large cash flow. The tenants pay off the mortgage, and the owner reaps the benefits of appreciation.

A portfolio with a mix of appreciation and cash flow investments is ideal, but it ultimately lies in your level of comfort and goals. Many people enter into this business with the sole reason of being rich, but unfortunately, once they encounter a few obstacles, they leave with a bitter and negative perspective of real estate. Like any profession, it has its positives and negatives, and in my experience, the positives outweigh the negatives. There is a reason why most wealthy people earned their wealth through real estate.

Chapter 4

PROPERTY HUNT!!!

Condominium- This is a great way for beginners to enter into real-estate investing. Condos can be purchased rent ready or as a fixer-upper. A fixer-upper condo typically requires cosmetic updates on the interior, while the condominium board maintains any exterior maintenance or repairs. A kitchen or bathroom update may be the largest renovation. As opposed to a single family home which will incur more costs to renovate, depending on the condition, and the interior and exterior have to be maintained. Also, vandalism is not a factor in a vacant condo as it is in a single family home.

However, do your due diligence when buying a condo. One of the first things you want to check is the assessment fees. Condo Assessment Fees or Homeowner Association Fees are the fees charged to each owner to maintain the condominium building. These fees may include items such as: lawn maintenance, snow removal, doorman, elevator maintenance, and utilities such as water, cable, etc. Find out what your assessment fees includes. If the assessment fees are too high, then you need to reassess your decision to purchase. The numbers may not be profitable for a rental or flipping. Flipping is buying a property below market value, adding value to the property and re-selling the property at or above market value for a profit.

It is imperative to ensure that the condominium association permits renters. Some condominium associations forbid renting the unit, this can limit your investing strategy. If you are flipping a condo, check to make sure the building qualifies for Federal Housing Administration (FHA) financing. This is extremely important because, if it is not eligible for FHA financing, this can limit your potential buyers from the buying pool. The limited buyers that would be eligible are cash buyers or those that qualify for conventional financing.

This may cause the unit to linger on the market for months and thus reduces your profit because of holding costs. Your real estate agent may request price reductions to entice buyers, all of which will ultimately lead to a smaller profit or none at all. By the way, you should always include holding costs in your buying analysis. Holding costs include mortgage payments, Homeowner Association (HOA) fees, utilities, property taxes and insurance.

BEWARE: Always inquire if there are any recent or looming special assessment fees. Special assessment fees are levied against all condo unit owners to pay for renovations or maintenance projects such as a new roof, boiler system, or plumbing and electrical updates, etc. Special assessments can limit the profitability of your deal. I spoke earlier in the book (preface) about my first condo purchase. Before my husband and I were set to close on the sale of our first condo, the condo association sent a letter notifying us of a special assessment for a new boiler system and exterior maintenance. The bill was over ten thousand dollars. It was disappointing, but needless to say we actually had to bring money to the closing just to close.

Single Family homes/Townhouses- Many investors begin their real estate career with Single Family Home (SFH), or townhouse rentals or flips. These are easier properties to purchase when getting your feet wet in real estate. Some investors prefer rent ready or turnkey properties, while some prefer to earn sweat equity and undertake a small or big renovation. Sweat equity is the non-financial investment that contributes to the development of a project/renovation, such as labor. An example would be painting the house yourself instead of hiring a professional. SFH, unlike condos, the exterior has to be maintained by the owner.

Moreover, if the property is located in a private community, then you may have to pay Homeowner Association fees and abide by the rules and regulations of the board. This should be taken into consideration before purchasing because it can hinder your design choices on the exterior of the property, if you plan to execute any projects on the exterior. Townhouses can be similar to apartments, in regards to complaints. I had a tenant renting a townhouse and the tenant complained about the noise and rodents of the neighboring unit.

Multifamily/Apartment Buildings (MFR)- These properties offer you the ability to live in your property while you collect rent. You can start small and purchase a two-flat or go big and acquire a 20-unit apartment. When the property has more than four units, it is considered commercial and requires commercial financing. Also, be mindful that depending on your local residential laws, you may have to contract a garbage pickup service if your building has more than four units. Landscaping and snow removal are other costs which you will incur. If you purchase a building with four-units or less, you can qualify for FHA financing, depending on your income and credit. If you are considering Section 8 tenants, HUD limits the number of Section 8 tenants per building. The building cannot be fully occupied by all Section 8 tenants. Have your agent verify that the utilities are separated for each unit. Also verify that the property has been classified as a multi-family. I've seen properties that have a multi-family layout but they are zoned as SFH. The biggest advantage of owning a multi-family, is the vacancy rate is lower because with a SFH investment property you are solely depending on one tenant for income. Whereas multifamily investment property is occupied by more than one tenant and this also allows you to earn more income from one asset.

Turnkey-Turnkey properties are properties that are rent ready; they require no repairs. These properties are great to acquire if you are an out-of-state investor or an investor that lacks the desire to rehab a property. These properties can be purchased on the open market, such as the MLS. However, there are companies that specialize in providing investors with turnkey properties. Some turnkey companies that sell these properties also offer property management services. If you purchase from one of these "turnkey" companies, make sure you visit the property, because many of these companies have been accused of false advertisement and selling junk. There are countless horror stories and lawsuits surrounding turnkey companies. Also, there is typically no equity in these properties. You are paying for someone else's equity, and the prices of these properties are listed at market rate or even higher.

Below is a lists of attributes that I try to identify when buying property. It is also inclusive of things that are undesirable to my real estate portfolio. This is a not a one-size-fits-all exhaustive list. It is incumbent on you to figure out what your lists of "no's" are and your "sweet spot." When my husband and I got started, we were literally horrified on seeing a house that was missing a toilet, and then it graduated to homes that needed roof replacements. Now we have experience with these repairs and others. We also have cultivated relationships with contractors we trust, and our lists of "no's" has decreased.

SWEET SPOT

SFH or a Multifamily property located within a one-block radius from a school, are easier to rent. The school's rating is not important because not every child can attend a top-performing school; that is why each community has neighborhood schools.

-Properties with backyards and fencing are attractive to most buyers and tenants with families.

-Investment properties with garages are always great, and side drives are the icing on the cake. I invest in Chicago. Winters can be brutal; buyers and tenants alike appreciate off-street parking.

-When buying property, be cognizant of the exterior maintenance costs the property will need. Stucco properties, in my experience, can be expensive to repair and maintain, depending on the geographical location and climate. Siding and brick are low-maintenance, but siding will need power washing and perhaps a new coat of paint every 10 to 15 years. A brick house will require tuck pointing every 25-30 years. I prefer brick homes over other building materials, because of the durability and low-maintenance.

-Three bedrooms or more in an SFH/MFR is desirable because you can charge more for rent. Also they attract long-term tenants.

That's a NO for me!

Flood Zones- Homes located in flood zones are extremely difficult to insure, and the premiums are exorbitant when you obtain flood insurance.

Basements that Flood- Properties that have been previously or currently flooded with rain-water are risky. This is not too be confused with seepage, but rather knee-deep water. If it's a rental property, this can pose legal and health risks and can be very expensive to remedy. In addition to having the tenants complain that their belongings were destroyed in a basement flood, even if you have forewarned them of the risk. The health issues that the tenant can suffer from mold and mildew in a basement can be severe. Also by law in most states, the landlord must remove the mold; this can be expensive. If the property is a flip, and you can acquire the property at a price that allows you to still be profitable after installing a waterproof basement system it may make financial sense.

Major fire damage- I have purchased a home that was involved in a small kitchen fire. It was a great deal and the home was located across the street from a school. The purchase price covered the costs of remediation. I would not purchase a home that was engulfed in a major fire.

Outrageous property taxes- ALWAYS verify the property taxes before you submit an offer and have your attorney check when the offer gets accepted. If it is a rental property, it may not be profitable if the taxes are too high to make any positive cash flow. If it is a flip, and the property taxes are much higher than surrounding properties, then it can present some challenges when its time to sell. This very thing happened to me. The listing agent advertised the property as having very low property taxes, but when my attorney prepared the closing costs figures, I noticed the taxes were double what was on the MLS. I still completed the purchase because it remained a positive cash flow deal, but just beware.

Mold- Homes that are covered in mold and require waivers to enter are off limits to me. The expense to resolve the mold and the health risks exceed my level of comfort.

Building Code Violations-Properties encumbered by building code violations are undesirable for me because of the time and money spent in housing court. The major governmental oversight these properties command is just not worth my energy. These properties can be a nightmare to repair.

Properties surrounded by abandoned or boarded up Properties- Avoid properties that are proximate to boarded-up properties. It is very challenging to find quality tenants that want to live next to a boarded up property, rented or owned. I made this mistake. Even as I was getting several showings on the property, and compliments on the interior, many potential tenants expressed concern about the boarded-up home next door and the safety issue it posed. Boarded up homes invite crime. These homes are an eyesore to the community.

Multifamily properties with tiny bedrooms- Multi-family properties with tiny bedrooms under 100 square feet can be difficult to rent. The only exception is if the location is experiencing a high demand for housing. Otherwise, I would suggest to continue your property search because, in my experience, tiny bedrooms are a major deal breaker for many renters.

One-bedroom Houses- A one-bedroom house can be very difficult to sell or rent, depending on your market. Normally these homes have awkward layouts, and appraisals can be relatively low on these homes because there aren't many similar comparable sales in the area. In most instances, you can pay the same price for two-bedrooms and get a larger rental rate than you would for a one-bedroom property.

FINANCING

Much like the strip club, in real estate, CASH is king. But if you don't have a pile of cash lying around, that's ok....you have options.

Cash- Paying cash in most instances will give you leverage over other buyers that bid with bank financing. Sometimes you can acquire the property at a discount because you have cash and close quickly. Cash allows you to purchase homes that are not financeable due to the condition of the property. However, after repairs these properties offer incredible equity that you can capitalize on. Even if you have access to cash, you can always leverage your money. Buy with cash, fix it up and do a cash-out refinance. Then, use the money to rinse and repeat on the next property.

*Hard Money Lenders-*These are private investors or companies that offer short-term lending to fund real estate deals. This type of lending is only recommended for flips, not for buy and hold strategies (i.e. rentals) unless you can refinance immediately. Typically, the interest rate is higher and the loan terms are 9-24 months.

Traditional bank loan, Conventional or FHA- An FHA loan is a great option if you buy an owner-occupied property between one to four units, depending on your credit, income, purchase price etc. FHA, offers low-down payments and competitive interests rates. This is a great way to break into real estate investing, particularly if you purchase a multifamily, because you can live in one unit and rent out the others. Generally, the rent covers the mortgage and allows you to save a downpayment or pay cash for another property. However, if you already own a primary residence, then the required downpayment may increase 10-30% on an investment property.

A 203k loan is a great option for properties that need repairs and can be financed. This is a renovation or construction loan backed by FHA. This loan is a hybrid of a standard FHA mortgage and home improvement loan allowing the buyer to borrow their renovation costs.

Conventional loans typically require a larger downpayment and a higher credit score than an FHA loan. These loans can be harder to qualify for and the interest rate may be higher than an FHA loan. However, the appraisal requirements for a conventional loan are less strict than FHA and other government backed loans.

Family/Friends-This is probably the last resort because of the complexities regarding family and money. Think long and hard when taking this approach, as this could potentially ruin a relationship. Thanksgiving dinner just doesn't taste the same (as Dave Ramsey would put it) when you owe Uncle Buck $10k on a deal that didn't go as successfully as planned. Remember, put everything in writing; sometimes people get amnesia about the terms and details of deals when money is involved.

Partner- Seeking a partner is another option if you have a skill set related to real estate and you lack the funding. Or you're really good at finding lucrative deals, this could also help attract a financial partner or a career in wholesaling real-estate. The partner could assist with funding the deal, while you do the repairs on the property, if you're handy or vice-versa. It is of the utmost importance that you get all the details in writing on how the profits will be split or if it doesn't sell Plan B. Finding a mutually beneficial partnership is key.

Owner Financing- Owner financing/land contracts are similar to a mortgage; but, rather than borrowing the money from a bank to buy the property, the buyer makes payments to the owner until the loan is paid in full or until the loan is refinanced. This is a great option, especially if you're struggling with credit issues or down payments. This financing also lends itself to be more creative. The interest rates are higher than bank institutions mortgage rates, but the terms are more flexible. There are not many sellers open to these agreements (few are) and you have to put in the time and energy to find them. Many times, sellers who offer owner-financing are older investors, aging out the business. They want to sell but still receive returns on their

money.

Chapter 5

OFFER, OFFER, OFFER

Once you have narrowed your search, identified lucrative deals, and lined up financing, it is then time to start writing offers. When you're submitting offers, again ALWAYS pay attention to the property taxes, building code violations, and association fees if any. It can make or break your deal.

Upon submitting offers, you must submit POF (proof of funds). This could be a bank statement if you're paying cash. If financing the property, a pre-approval from a bank or a hard-money lender will do. Also, the real estate agent will ask how much you want to offer as an earnest money deposit. This is traditionally 10% of the offer price. Earnest money is a deposit to the seller from the buyer to demonstrate good faith in a transaction. I once read an article about a successful real estate investor, and he offered this piece of advice, when submitting low ball offers, "if you're not embarrassed about the offer, it is not low enough."

When you are submitting offers on investment properties, it is common practice to place bids on several properties to see which one sticks. Make sure that these are properties that actually make financial sense, just in case your offer is accepted. You want to establish a good reputation, part of that is being able to complete the deal. Realtors work harder for you when you are serious and have established a pattern of closing deals. More deals will come to you because of your good follow-through reputation.

Investor Tip: If you're feeling confident about the deal and the numbers work well, offer a large earnest money deposit — say 50-75% of the offered price. This will convey your seriousness to the seller. This will assure the seller that you can close the deal, and it gives you a competitive edge over other buyers. In my experience of doing this, my offer is accepted. But only do this if you are completely certain of the deal and the financing because you do not want to jeopardize your earnest money deposit. If you are considering placing an offer on a property occupied by tenants, request a copy of the lease and pay attention to the security deposits.

Make sure the security deposit is included in the purchase, and inquire about photos or video of what the unit or property looked like before the tenants moved in. Check to see if the tenants are up-to-date on the rent. Acquiring tenants with a property can be challenging, but it can also be an advantage because you can start collecting rent immediately. Another strategy experienced investors use is waiving the inspection contingency in the purchase contract. You can bring an inspector or contractor to the first or second showing. Hiring an inspector to accompany on the first or second showing to inspect the property will allow you to proceed, without the inspection contingency, thereby giving you an edge above other bidders.

It is pertinent to analyze the numbers and have a decent grasp of the pricing and demographics of your particular investing area. Here are some questions to help determine if it is better to rent or flip the property.

1. Is this area populated by homeowners or renters? Areas that are highly populated by renters don't usually work well for flipping because the ARV (after repair value) may yield smaller profit margins. This is because most of the sales in the area will reflect purchases from investors buying them at discounted rates to rent them. Also, this demographic may not qualify for a mortgage.

2. What is the median income? This is important because if the median income in the area is low, perhaps below $30,000, then this demographic may have a more difficult time qualifying for a mortgage.

3. Are the school systems ranked well? Most people want to live in an area that has a great school system if they have, or are planning on having, children. Good school systems generally accompany higher housing costs because demand for the community will increase the price of homes. If you find a good deal within a good school community you're on the right track. This may present a great flipping opportunity.

4. What is the crime rate? Crime-ridden neighborhoods tend to have lower home selling values. However, the rent values may be quite profitable. These neighborhoods are mostly comprised of renters.

5. Average price of homes that have been rehabbed and sold. If you find a good deal, make sure your realtor creates a CMA report, that way you can analyze your profit with ac-

curate numbers. A CMA or comparative market analysis is an evaluation of similar recently sold homes in a particular neighborhood.

Chapter 6

TENANT PROOF

If you purchased a property that needs improvements, or you want to incorporate upgrades to the property which could increase the longevity of the building materials, (such as flooring to cabinets). Here are a few tips:

Rehabbing

Rehabbing a property can be both fun and stressful. Obtain the appropriate permits and ensure that your contractor is licensed. There are some do-it-yourself projects that you can tackle if you're looking to save money or just gain experience on renovating. I highly recommend shopping and choosing the materials for the rehab. This experience will give you a good idea of the prices and selection of materials that are available. Salespeople in the stores can recommend certain products that may be better suited for renting vs flipping. Also, this knowledge will assist you on your next real estate purchase, as you will know accurate costs of materials rather than guesstimates or inaccurate figures you've seen on home improvement reality shows. If you're not handy but want to tackle a few small projects, YouTube is your friend. This is another area where you can capitalize on your equity.

Also, when you receive quotes from contractors, you will gain more knowledge about the scope of the work, i.e., the time and labor costs, because you can compare the quotes. Example: If you want a quote to replace a toilet, and one estimate from a plumber charges $500, while the other quotes are $150-$200, then this will provide you with realistic numbers for your budget. When you're getting started in this business, gaining knowledge on all facets of real estate will help you increase your chances of becoming successful in the future. There are many ways to be duped and lose lots of money in this business, so arm yourself with as much knowledge as possible to appear somewhat informed about the rehab process, lest you be scammed.

When dealing with contractors that you neither know or were not referred, check their licensing and insurance. Insist on references along with some pictures of their previous work. Make sure you get everything in writing that describes the scope of the work, along with the date of commencement and the date of completion. If you can, try to include a penalty clause in the contract that will incentivize the contractor to complete the work in a timely matter. If the contractor is planning on using subcontractors for the job, then document their names and ensure they are covered under the contractors insurance policy. Try to be present at the job site as much as possible.

When the contractor receives final payment for the job, always write final payment in the check memo and have the contractor and his subs sign a contractor lien waiver. A lien waiver is a legal document for a contractor or subcontractor stating they have received full payment and waive any future lien rights to the property. Consult your attorney for this document. This will prevent a contractor or a subcontractor from trying to place a mechanics lien on your property. A mechanics lien is a legal remedy that contractors or subcontractors utilize when they have not been compensated for the labor or materials on a property they worked on. If a court grants the lien, the judgment amount will be placed against your house to recover the money. Even if you paid the general contractor, if he/she failed to pay the subcontractors they can legally pursue a mechanics lien.

NEVER give cash without receiving a receipt. Remember, "People's Court" Judge Milian says a crayon and a napkin will suffice, so just get it in writing.

Contractor Tip: Hiring contractors that have a day job in the field of which you're employing him/her can be advantageous to your budget. For instance, hiring an electrician that works for a large electrical company like, ComEd, but works independently on side jobs. They will generally charge cheaper rates, since this is not how they derive their sole source of income.

EXAMPLE:

UNCONDITIONAL WAIVER AND RELEASE ON FINAL PAYMENT

NOTICE TO CLAIMANT: THIS DOCUMENT WAIVES AND RE-LEASES LIEN, STOP PAYMENT NOTICE, AND PAYMENT BOND RIGHTS UNCONDITIONALLY AND STATES THAT YOU HAVE BEEN PAID FOR GIVING UP THOSE RIGHTS. THIS DOCUMENT IS EN-FORCEABLE AGAINST YOU IF YOU SIGN IT, EVEN IF YOU HAVE NOT BEEN PAID. IF YOU HAVE NOT BEEN PAID, USE A CONDI-TIONAL WAIVER AND RELEASE FORM.

CONTRACT PARTIES INFORMATION

Name of Claimant:_____

Name of Customer:_____

Job Location:_____

Owner:_____

Conditional Waiver and Release

This document waives and releases lien, stop payment notice, and payment bond rights the claimant has for all labor and service provided, and equipment and material delivered, to the customer on this job. Rights based upon labor or service provided, or equipment or material delivered, pursuant to a written change order that has been fully executed by the parties prior to the date that this document is signed by the claimant, are waived and released by this document, unless listed as an Exception below. The claimant has been paid in full.

Exceptions

This document does not affect any of the following:

Disputed claims for extras in the Amount of:
$_____

Signature

CONTRACTOR Signature:_____

CONTRACTOR Title:_____

Date of Signature:_____

Security-Wireless alarm systems have become popular and it allows you to monitor a vacant property and arm the system without being present. ADT is not your only option for security. One such system is SimpliSafe. These companies don't require any long-term contracts. Moreover, there are some contractors that will live on the property while they rehab it. Usually the contractor will offer a discounted rate for the work since they will be receiving free housing. Another option is dogs. Some contractors will keep Pit bulls, Rottweilers, or other intimidating breeds in the home to discourage burglars.

BEWARE: Some towns or cities will require that you register your property if it is vacant. These fees can add up. For instance, in Chicago, vacant SFH require a $250 fee and proof of an insurance policy of $300,000 in personal liability. If you fail to do so, the fine doubles and you have to attend a court hearing.

Exterior Painting- Choose a neutral color or one that blends with the neighborhood when painting the exterior.

If you are unsure of your choice, ask an expert. Visit a paint store, such as Benjamin Moore or Sherwin Williams; they can give you advice and even ideas on color combinations. When I purchased my first SFH, it was beige. I wanted to revive the exterior, but I chose an awful royal blue. The store's employees and the painters I hired to paint the house tried to deter me, but I couldn't be saved, for I knew everything...*sighs.* When I was ready to re-sell, buyers were repulsed by the icky blue shade color of the house. Ultimately, I had to pay for it to be painted back to beige and then it sold.

Furnace- I recommend hiring a well-known established company when you are replacing a furnace or a/c unit. These appliances can costs thousands of dollars and you want to ensure that it will be under warranty by a reputable company that stands by its service and products for the life of the appliance. I attempted to save money and allowed a guy that repaired furnaces as a side gig to install a new furnace in one of my properties. Well, when the situation ended on a sour note, he refused to service the unit. My only recourse is to contact the manufacturer, but I still have to pay a repairman to install the parts. Don't be like me; use a reputable company. When maintaining your furnace for your rentals, be sure to use 90-Day furnace filters. It will correspond with your quarterly inspections. In the past, I relied on tenants to change the furnace filters, but I discovered that repairs would increase on the furnace so I wouldn't encourage you to delegate this chore to the tenants.

Thermostats- Reconsider upgrading your manual thermostat to a digital thermostat on a rental property. Digital thermostats are great for flips. However, I received many complaints from tenants who struggle with operating the digital thermostat. Most digital thermostats require batteries and some tenants would use cheap off-brand batteries which would cause the thermostat to die frequently. This would lead to frantic calls of furnace breakdowns, when it was merely the thermostat batteries. Digital thermostats are designed for energy efficiency, but some tenants mistake it for a furnace malfunction. Anyway, do yourself a favor and keep the manual thermostat. For multifamily properties, install a lock on each thermostat and keep the heat at 68 degrees during the winter or the minimum temperature your local laws mandate.

A/C units-There is a nationwide epidemic of A/C units being stolen for the precious copper inside. The thieves sell them to scrap metal companies for cash. It is really important to install cages on an a/c unit because they are expensive to replace between ($1500-$5000). If your property is vacant, it is very important to have a safety device, because you become a target for theft and vandalism.

I recently had this situation occur. I was buying a property, and during the final walk through I noticed the a/c unit was stolen. My realtor reported it to the bank. It was a HUD property and they took nearly three weeks to counter back with a $250 credit. Needless to say, by that time thieves had started removing other things from the property, I walked away from the deal. But the lesson is that if you have an a/c unit on a rental property, you should invest in an a/c unit security cage. The property recently closed and the bank received $6k less than our contract price.

Ceiling Fans/Light fixtures- In my experience, it's really important that you invest in light bulb friendly fixtures for rental properties. Simplified: make sure the tenant doesn't have to remove any covers or contraptions that make it difficult to change a light bulb. I have received endless amounts of service call requests for light bulb changes because the fixture requires a screw driver to replace the bulb.

Kitchen Cabinets- If you are replacing the kitchen cabinets on a rental property, choose a darker color cabinetry, laminate or oak cabinetry has proven to be durable and affordable. ALWAYS, install knobs on the cabinets, it contributes to the longevity of the cabintets. If you are flipping, then consider visiting other flips in the neighborhood to familiarize yourself with the trends or visit a home-improvement showroom.

Wall Fixtures- Wall fixtures, such as toilet paper handles and towel bars, are greatly discouraged in low-income rental properties. These fixtures among this tenant class mostly end up torn off the wall. The holes for the fixture become bigger, and you end up with a repair. The key is to minimize potential repairs and the amount of holes in the walls.

Tile- Everyone raves that ceramic tile is a durable product for rentals, but in my experience, over time, the tenant can cause cracks in the tiles. It can be a nuisance to replace and if you're renting to a Section 8 tenant, cracked tile can result in a housing violation. This could, in turn, result in loss of rent. Repairing tile while the property is occupied can be challenging to say the least. The only place I recommend tile is in bathrooms and backslashes.

I recommend a darker grout, for tiling, because from experience, white/beige grout even when it is sealed, tends to look dirty and dingy after a couple of years or even a year — depending on the tidiness of your tenant. Be sure to use darker tiles, as lighter tiles are difficult to keep clean. Tiles that have patterns tend to maintain their attractiveness after years of wear and tear. Detailed tiling can be a great selling feature for flips.

Paint color- Utilizing the same paint color saves you time. Choose a light tone but in the tan hues. NEVER use flat paint in a rental property, as this paint is not conducive to wear and tear. It will require you to repaint the entire house each time a tenant moves out. Consider an eggshell or semi-gloss, as stains wipe off easier. ANYTHING but flat! I love to save money, when I first started I would always use cheap generic paint. It would take several coats for good coverage, but I was enamored with $10 price tag for a gallon of paint, #winning. I was fooling myself, for the money I saved from buying cheap paint it costs more in the amount of labor and time to paint a room. To sum it up, use a good brand, my favorite brands are BEHR and Glidden paint.

Appliances- I always purchase new appliances for my rentals. I know some landlords like to purchase used appliances, but the goal is to minimize service calls. I enjoy the peace of mind that comes with knowing there is a warranty on the appliance and I receive the full life expectancy on that new appliance. Check your local hardware store for sales and clearance deals. Sometimes Sears Outlet and Best Buy clearance department have good deals on appliances as well.

As a caveat, if you include laundry appliances in your rental agreement, then have an additional addendum in your lease that states that the appliances are "as-is" and repairs or maintenance are the responsibility of the tenant. If it is an apartment with a community laundry room consider purchasing coin-operated washer and dryers; this may increase your profits. Lastly, make sure you have a lint trap connected to the washing machine plumbing. If you neglect to use a lint trap, then it can cause back-ups and clogs in your plumbing system; this will lead to expensive plumbing bills. Change them quarterly.

Talk to the neighbors-Don't be shy; if you see your neighbors, then introduce yourself. Give them your card, and encourage them to call if they see or hear anything suspicious. Most people welcome rehabbers; because they are improving the neighborhood. One of the most rewarding things for me in this business is when neighbors comment and tell me how much they love the new curb appeal I've added to the block. No one wants to live next to a boarded-up home. It brings down the value of the surrounding homes, and it may invite criminals or trespassers. You are doing a good service to the community.

Bathrooms-Bathroom renovations can be expensive to renovate. If you have a sturdy tub that is just dingy, it may be cost-effective to have the tub professionally refinished, which usually runs about $250-$300. The result is a beautiful glossy white tub. Make sure to follow the care instructions well, and give a copy to the tenant and reiterate the care instructions verbally. Also, if you have intact bathroom or kitchen tiles on the wall, the tile glazing refinishing process is a great cost/time efficient option. Tiling can be very expensive, as the materials and labor can add up quickly. This follows for replacing tubs; you could be opening up a can of worms by removing a functional tub. This could lead to expensive plumbing bills and a lengthy delay for plumbing permits.

Vacant insurance-This is a must-have if you buy the property vacant, even if the property is turn-key. This policy will protect your investment, until you fill the vacancy. This advice is more suited for cash buyers because banks do not finance properties without insurance in place before closing. If you are rehabbing a vacant property and you have a landlord rental insurance policy on the property, then most insurance companies will not cover you because it is vacant. Vacant insurance policies offer coverage for homes that are being rehabbed and or have no occupants. The policy is very inexpensive, usually about $200-$500 for six months, and you can renew if you have not completed the project within that time. Ask your local insurance agent about a vacant insurance policy. Remember to switch to a traditional landlord policy when the property becomes occupied, because the vacant policy would no longer apply.

Interior Doors-If you're renting to a low-income demographic and you are replacing the interior doors of the unit, I strongly suggest an oak or a brown color door. White doors can be a nightmare because they will either require thorough cleaning when the tenant moves out or re-painting. Either way, it's a hassle. Stick to door colors that camouflage stains and wear and tear.

Laminate Flooring- I love laminate hardwood flooring for my rental properties. However, I suggest buying a higher quality laminate 12mm or higher because 8mm and under may not be as durable and sturdy. When choosing a laminate, also consider the color. A light or golden oak is good because it hides nicks and scratches while a very dark color laminate will show every nick and scratch in the material. Select colors that are more forgiving of the normal wear and tear in rental units. Laminate flooring is also great for flipping, depending on the demographic of buyers.

Hardwood Flooring-Buyers, low-income and affluent tenants love hardwood floors. These are a great selling feature for homes that you want to flip. Buff them and make them shine. If you are renting, require a generous security deposit, just in case they are damaged during the tenancy.

Countertops-Laminate countertops have come a long way. The big box stores now offer many styles and selections to update the look of your kitchen on a modest budget. They are easy to install and range from $20-$100. I strongly suggest you choose darker colors or patterned countertops for rentals. These will be more forgiving of stains and wear and tear. Marble, granite, and other high end stones are great for flips. Some flippers even use granite countertops in low-income markets, because they are so popular among buyers. And many landlords choose this product for affluent renters.

Winterize-Winterize the property if you live in a cold-climate, especially if it's vacant. This process will eliminate pipe-bursting fiascos. The process is fairly simple and will save you thousands of dollars. If you purchase a foreclosure property in the winter, it is likely winterized by the bank, to protect there investment. The orange or lime green stickers/notices of winterization can be found in the kitchen, bath, and basement — anywhere the plumbing fixtures are located. If it is purchased by a traditional seller, definitely winterize if you don't intend to turn on the heating utilities. Seek the assistance of a plumber to winterize your property.

Carpet-If you choose carpet, then avoid light colors unless it is a flip. For rentals, I recommend brown, grey, or navy. These colors are more forgiving of stains.

Lastly, in the beginning of your real estate investing career, you may wear many hats. However, you must learn to delegate as your portfolio grows. If you try to remain a one-man/woman show, then you may burn out and not survive the longevity of this business. Therefore, building a team to support your dream is imperative. Building systems within your real estate business can be very advantageous to the success of your business. Systems will help you estimate the costs of a rehab before you bid on the property:

Here's an example: After several real estate transactions, whether renting or selling, it is easier to use the same materials for all your projects. That would entail, documenting the Stock Keeping Unit (SKU)/serial number for ceiling fans, faucets, flooring, etc. Don't get enticed by those reality flipping shows that show the investor shopping for different fixtures and flooring for each house they purchase; it's not realistic. Also, it is particularly helpful for landlords when all of your properties have uniformity regarding fixtures, cabinets, flooring, etc. It's easier to repair and replace things, and you also observe the durability of the products you choose and adjusts accordingly.

Chapter 7

FINDING A TENANT

The ideal tenant has job stability, preferably a career, with two years or more in the profession. The income should be 3x the monthly rent. Example: Rent is $1000/monthly, so the tenant should have a net monthly income of $3000 or more. Anything less than that is a risk. They should have a credit score of 700 or better, but the threshold I typically use for low-income tenants is 600 minimum credit score.

The criteria may vary depending on the demographic of the neighborhood. The tenant should have a clean criminal background, which includes NO felonies. The good people at BRAVO and VH1 like felons, but I can't take those risks. NO evictions. Tenants that have previously owned a home make really great tenants because they have previous experience with maintaining a house. Another desirable attribute is a tenant with good cleaning habits and a quiet lifestyle. Tenants that take the initiative to troubleshoot a problem before calling the landlord are very desirable. These, in a nutshell, are some of the qualities you want to identify when you are meeting with prospective tenants. This lists below will assists you in choosing a model tenant.

So you're ready to list your property for RENT!

Finding the right tenant can be a process. If you prefer, you can enlist the help of a real estate agent. They will list the property on the MLS. They have a network within their profession with access to a wide range of tenants. Typically they charge the price of the rent, for example: if the rent is

$900, their fee will be $900. This fee entails showing the property, screening and processing the paperwork, etc. For some investors hiring a realtor to fill the vacancy, makes sense for them financially and time-wise. Here's the caveat, you need to screen the agent and their screening process. The last thing you want is an inexperienced real estate agent choosing the first tenant who walks through the door without doing the proper screening, and they get paid and you end up with a nightmarish tenant. Here is a short list of questions you should ask the real estate agent.

1. Where do you advertise to find tenants?

2. What is the length of time it takes you to fill a vacancy?

3. What is your screening process?

4. What is your monthly income requirement for rent?

5. Do you consider landlord references?

6. How do you determine the rent amount for the property?

7. How many comparable properties do you consider?

8. What days will you be available to show the property?

If you have chosen to hire a property manager to fill the vacancy and manage the rental property, the questions should be more in-depth:

1. How long do you retain your average tenant?

2. How many units do you manage? This is important because a really large management company sometimes neglect mom-and-pop small rental portfolios.

3. How do you collect rent? Do they enforce late fees?

4. How many tenants have you evicted in the past year? If the number is relatively high in proportion to the units they manage, then they have a poor screening process.

5. Are they familiar with the landlord/tenant laws and ordinances in your area?

6. Ask about their eviction policy.

7. What fees do they charge for an eviction?

8. How do they handle security deposits?

9. How do they handle service calls?

10. What are the fees for repairs from service calls?

11. How often do they conduct inspections?

DIY

If you decided to list the property and forgo any assistance. Here are a few common places most landlords post their rental listing.

1. Zillow Rental Manager website. This is my go-to website when advertising a unit for rent. This gives your listing the most exposure because it is seen on Zillow, Trulia, and Hotpads — as well as all of their partner websites.

2. Craigslist. Posting here is fine; just beware of scammers on this site.

3. Local stores and shops in your area, if they have a bulletin board.

4. Word of Mouth.

5. If you have a property in a big city or in a tourist area, you may want to consider Airbnb. This is for short-term leases, but it can be very lucrative. If you select this option, research any ordinances in your town or city that may affect your ability to advertise or rent to Airbnb guests. Some big cities, like Chicago, have placed very restrictive ordinances and high fees and taxes on hosts that advertise on Airbnb.

6. www.socialserve.com a website dedicated to providing housing to renters with housing vouchers.

THERE'S NO CHILLIN' WITHOUT SCREENIN'

Screening tenants is of the utmost importance. There should be a heavy emphasis on screening. This will allow you to enjoy a leisurely lifestyle. Good quality tenants make your life easier. Before we delve into the screening process, let's do a brief lesson on housing discrimination. Federal law prohibits housing discrimination based on race, color, national origin, religion, sex, familial status, or disability. Therefore, when you are screening a potential applicant, none of the aforementioned conditions can be taken into consideration. Mmkay?..OK!

When your phone begins to ring with prospective tenants, you will be tempted to show the property to the first person that expresses interests. Hold your horses; you've got an interrogation to conduct... I mean screening to do. If you receive a call from a Section 8 voucher holder, NEVER say you don't accept Section 8. It is against the law, and it is considered housing discrimination. Here are some questions that you must ask over the phone to distinguish those that meet your criteria. Your TIME is valuable.

1. What is your move-in date?

2. Why are you moving?

3. What's your income?

4. How many people will be living in the unit?

5. How many animals? If so, what kind?

6. Do you smoke?

7. What do you do for a living? How long have you been employed at your job?

8. Will you have a security deposit and first month's rent upon move-in?

9. Have you ever been evicted?

10. Are you a Section 8 voucher holder? Inquire about the monthly portion they are currently paying. I have seen situations where the tenant pays a large portion, say $900/monthly. On the other hand, there are some tenants that pay a $0/monthly portion and Section 8 covers the entire monthly rent of the unit. In the cases

where tenants pay larger portions, you may want to weigh the risk. One of the benefits of renting to a Section 8 tenant is receiving guaranteed rent. However, this option may be less appealing if you have to try to collect a large portion of rent from the Section 8 tenant while also adhering to all the Section 8 regulations. Having said that, you cannot deny a prospective tenant based on their portion unless they fail to provide proof of income to pay their portion.

These questions are your criteria for approving an applicant. If a prospective applicant fails to meet the basic qualifications, it is a moot point to show the property. For instance, I met a prospective tenant at a property that was fully renovated. She loved the property and requested an application. I inquired if she had any pets, she had a dog. I have a no pet policy. This was both a waste of her time and mine.

Showing Process

1. Rental applications- These are standard forms which can be printed off the internet for free. You should have at least ten, on hand when you are showing the property. This form should include: full name, phone number, social security number, occupation, income, landlord references, and names of all parties that will occupy the unit. The application fee generally ranges from $25-$50. This covers the costs of the screening service and your time.

2. Receipt Book/Pen-Bring a receipt book for applicants that want to pay the application fee. Receipts provide a professional appearance.

3. When showing the property, guide the tour. Do not allow the prospective tenant/tenants to roam; this is for safety reasons. They could unlock a window or a basement door and if they come as a group, one could stray and hide in a bedroom closet or attic, etc. When you are

going up the stairs or going into the basement, allow the tenant to walk in front of you. Most people you encounter are seeking housing, but there is a chance you could encounter someone with nefarious intentions. Be careful and trust your instincts. Always let someone know your whereabouts. These types of crimes are not isolated to Lifetime Movies.

4. It is important that when you are showing the property and during the lease signing, you stress the property is "as-is." I can't tell you the endless requests and upgrades that tenants would ask for after they've moved in. Emphasize that what you see is what you get. If it is not suitable for them, then they should look elsewhere. These requests run the gamut of minor things like a doorbell, which I provide, but some of the requests can be expensive — such as replacing the screen door with a security door or repainting the entire first floor to another color at my expense, notwithstanding the entire house was newly painted. I've had requests to have all

the bedroom doorknobs replaced with doorknobs that locked; those are unreasonable requests. The most outrageous requests was for bars to be installed on all the windows. This was immediately denied because it is a safety violation. It was very unusual, given the property was located in a decent neighborhood and a block away from the police station. I also mailed a certified letter in writing warning them not to install bars on any windows.

Trust and Verify

Once you receive an application along with the fee, the next step is to process the information for criminal and credit history. The screening service I use is SmartMove, a subsidiary of TransUnion. The unique feature about this service is that they analyze the applicant for you based on credit, background and income. They will either recommend decline or accept an applicant. This is highly recommended for new landlords. In addition to using the screening process, you want to verify the references. This is really important, because many landlords skip this process.

First, call the current or past landlord on the application. When you call, ensure you are speaking to the actual landlord. Your call should start like this: "Hello, do you have any apartments available?"..if the caller is stumped or tells you it's a wrong number, the applicant is being deceitful and did not think you would verify this information. This is a red flag. If it is worth it to you, call the tenant and confirm the phone number. Move on if it is the same number. Here are a few questions you should ask the current or former landlord:

1. How much was the rent?

2. How long was the tenancy?

3. Did the tenant pay on time?

4. Would you rent to them again?

5. How did the tenant leave the unit?

6. How was the housekeeping?

These questions should give you clarity on the tenant. If you are pleased with the responses, the next step is verifying employment and income. After verifying this information, you should be able to make an informed, wise decision. If you choose the tenant, follow up to set up a meeting to review the lease; however, if you decide to decline the applicant, follow up with a letter in writing with your reasons for declining the applicant. Treat everyone with professionalism and uniformity.

Chapter 8

THE REJECTS

Below you will find a list of things to beware of when choosing a tenant that does not violate housing discrimination laws.

Red Flags, A.K.A, Thats a NO for me DAWG...(in my Randy Jackson voice).

***Past Evictions*-**It is my opinion that you should never accept a rental candidate that has an eviction on their credit report. It does not matter how old the eviction is. I have gone down this path, and it was a very stressful time. The tenant reverted back to her bad habits and offered every excuse to avoid her obligation to pay rent. When her tenancy ended, which I was on the brink of filing an eviction before she left; it caused me several thousand dollars to repair a property that was completely rehabbed prior to her moving in and loss of rent.

Clean Car Tests-Many landlords like to use this qualifier to get some insight into the applicants cleaning habits when screening tenants. After meeting with the applicant, the landlord will insist on walking the prospective tenant out to their car to observe if the car is tidy or looks like a garbage dump.

Complaining- If an applicant is bad mouthing their current/past landlord, proceed with caution. Although some of their complaints may be valid, this could also be a sign that this tenant would be difficult to please. This also applies if they are making complaints about the property at the showing, I can bet my good liver that this tenant will never be happy and will inflict unnecessary stress onto you just for kicks.

Lawsuits-If an applicant ever reveals they have sued a former landlord, or if it is revealed on the credit report, run for the hills. This lease will likely end with you as the defendant in court. I had a couple that passed the screening process, and when we met to sign the lease, the husband mentioned that they were in the midst of a lawsuit with their current landlord. Needless to say, that meeting didn't end with a signed lease.

Be'be's kids- This is another factor that should not be overlooked. If the children are hanging off the stair railings, running through the house and displaying other unruly behaviors, take note because they will probably not respect the property. Especially if this goes without reprimand from an adult. Also, applicants that show up with unkempt children (hair uncombed, dirty clothes, inappropriately dressed for the weather, etc.) are also considered risky. If they can't prioritize the cleanliness of their children, then it is highly likely they won't prioritize taking care of your property.

Bargain Hunters- If the applicant attempts to negotiate the deposit or discusses paying the deposit in increments after they move in, this candidate likely isn't in the position to afford the rent. I can bet my children's college tuition fund you will never see the full security deposit once the tenant moves in. It also sets a precedent for what you're willing to accept during the tenancy. Giving the tenant a payment plan for the security deposit reeks of desperation and tenants generally, take advantage of the kindness of desperate landlords. This is one of the things you do not want to waiver on. This also applies to applicants who balk or try to negotiate the application fee. Perspective, if you can't afford the application fee, then you probably can't afford the rent. Sometimes, potential applicants will complain that they have paid several application fees on their apartment search. I sympathize, but you must be consistent with the screening process.

Too many occupants- A prospective tenant that arrives to a showing appointment with an entire group of adults, but only one adult is on the lease, is a red flag. This can be an indication of unauthorized tenants, and possibly a fire hazard. There are housing laws that regulate the number of occupants that can legally reside in a house/apartment based on bedroom size or square footage. In the event a fire occurs, with several unauthorized tenants living there it may give the appearance of a slumlord and you may face penalties from the local government. Also, if eviction ever becomes an issue, it will become a long arduous process because of the number of people that will be affected by homelessness, if evicted. Judges have soft spots for these cases, and you will be vilified.

Late Arrivals- If you have an appointment and the applicant arrives 15 minutes or later without calling to forewarn you, or they show up without an apology, the applicant is not considerate of your time. This behavior may carry over when it's time to pay rent.

Belligerent behavior- If a potential applicant is arguing with their partner at the showing or perhaps cursing or speaking nasty towards their children, you might be next in line to feel their wrath. If they are not respectful towards the people closest to them, they will have no problem cursing you out. The goal is to secure quality tenants. One of the attributes of a quality tenant is he/she is a respectful level-headed person. If a problem occurs; like a leak, or a major appliance fails, then you don't want to have to deal with a verbally abusive tenant that refuses to acknowledge the efforts you are making to remedy the problem.

Immature- I rent mostly SFH. When I first got started, I had very loose standards and I would rent to anyone with a heart-beat, even those who still requiring more parenting. I rented one of my homes to a young teenage mom. She demanded a lot of my time and management services; it was difficult for her to manage a house. She was unfamiliar with operating a single family home, and she was more suited for an apartment. There were numerous plumbing issues because she would flush feminine products down the toilet, and her children would flush toys down, regardless of all the warnings and chiding. One of the most peculiar phone calls I've ever had was this particular tenant calling me about contracting the services of a mold remediation company because it was mold in the toilet. Toilet cleaner and a toilet brush was her mold remediation. She obviously assumed a maid service was complimentary with the property. Maybe this tenant was on the extreme side of a younger renter, but it was quite an experience. I'm not suggesting you discriminate towards anyone based on age, but some tenants require a micro-managing approach due to the lack of experience in living on their own.

Flashy Ashley- Beware of applicants that offer a large sum of cash upfront; I mean a BIG wad of cash that makes you feel like a rapper in a nightclub. This will likely be the last rent payment you receive once they move in. These individuals are usually unemployed and are not "quality" tenants. They are seeking desperate landlords that are willing to forgo the screening process in lieu of quick cash. These types are often professional tenants that know the housings laws and systems better than a HUD attorney.

Hasty-Applicants that are in a rush to move into the property can also be a sign of trouble. There are some legitimate situations where the tenant needs to move asap, say job relocation. However, this can be indicative of a person stiffing their current landlord on rent or in the process of being evicted. Think about it: do you want someone that has not given the proper notice of lease termination to their current landlord to reside in your property? You may find yourself in their shoes in a year or less.

Applicants that are rude or pushy-Attracting good people that show consideration and good manners make for great business relationships. Tenants can make or break your business; they can be an ally or an enemy. Sometimes personalities just don't mesh well from the beginning. Remember, this is very much like a partnership. You have to communicate with this person. If they are giving you resistance or an attitude during the screening process, I would suggest you halt the process entirely and move on to another serious applicant.

Don't allow strong personalities or control freaks steer the process on their terms. You have to set a standard in the beginning; otherwise, this will be a contentious partnership that will end in lawsuits and judgments. Here's an example: The applicant doesn't want to pay the application fee, (this is the fee you charge for doing a credit and eviction background check as well as verifying employment and personal references), but insists on giving you a copy of their current credit report. This is unacceptable, for this is one of the steps in the screening system that is non-negotiable. Do not compromise. There are some things you must not waiver on. Once the applicant realizes that you have compromised on that step, it will not end there. The trail of requests will be continued.

Home Visits- Once you have accepted an application and you are close to approving an applicant, some landlords like to visit the property of the potential tenant, in order to see how they live. I have done this on a few occasions; it will give you insight on their cleaning habits. This visit is not scheduled, but rather an impromptu meeting. You call and let them know you are in the area and need a document signed. The condition of the property should help you with your decision.

The lists of attributes that I have described above are the ingredients of a professional tenant. If you live in a tenant-friendly state like I do, you want to avoid renting to a professional tenant like Trump avoids taxes. These are the worse types of tenants; they are playing for keeps. They are usually aiming for one of two things: a monetary judgement from a judge based on a housing violation such as a security deposit, or, they want to stay in your property for an unlimited amount of time rent-free. If you have a mortgage this can ruin your credit, assuming you are unable to pay the mortgage while you have a squatter. The legal fees that result from these cases can lead to bankruptcy. Some courts have even mandated that landlords pay the legal fees of the tenant.

Some landlords give up on this career and sell their inventory because they have been so negatively affected by a professional tenant. It can be financially devastating...YOU'VE BEEN WARNED!! If possible, avoid applicants that have been on government assistance for longer than five years. These tenants, in my experience, abuse the program and know all the loopholes to use against you — should you enforce your lease in ways in which they do not agree. Example: I rented to a Section 8 tenant. When she moved in, it was her and three children. After a month her boyfriend moved in; I was not pleased and he was a sketchy character. I sent a written notice that she had violated her lease. She had 30 days to remedy the situation or face eviction.

Immediately, I began getting several calls from the housing department for "safety violations." I found myself encumbered in erroneous inspections and dealing with a very spiteful tenant. She was very unpleasant to deal with, she threatened me with bodily harm on numerous occasions, and even her children were belligerent towards me. I noticed the unit was being destroyed. There was cracked tile, missing kitchen cabinet doors and roaches — it was a nightmare. This tenant would call the housing department and report there was mold in the basement. I would then send a mold remediation company out to resolve the "mold." The mold company never found any mold just dirt, which vindicated me. Months later, I was able to prove through photos and other documentation that the tenant had moved in an "unapproved tenant." Eventually the tenant was threatened with losing her Section 8 voucher if she continued to allow her boyfriend to occupy the unit, so she moved. However, it was a very tumultuous time and costs me thousands of dollars to repair the property damage.

Ultimately, set standards do not deviate from those standards and be consistent with everyone. The last thing you want is to be accused of housing discrimination. By the way, I've been accused of that as well and received a call from the good people at HUD. I was renting a property in the suburbs, and the taxes were very high. I was delinquent on one statement. I received a call from a potential applicant inquiring if I accepted Section 8. I told her "no" but explained the reason was because the taxes were not current and they would have to be paid in full in order to rent to a Section 8 tenant. This caller was still irate and I ended the phone call. Three hours later, I receive a phone call from HUD regarding an accusation of housing discrimination. I explained my situation to the gentleman over the phone and the case was closed. Again, always say you accept Section 8, regardless of the circumstances.

Chapter 9

LEASES

If you are not using an attorney when constructing a residential lease, then search online for your local Realtors association residential lease. They offer free up-to-date leases that include local ordinances for your town. Example: www.chicagorealtor.com. Here are a few of the things I like to include in my leases.

Late Fees-These are standard in most residential leases. Avoid implementing outrageous late fees. Most housing courts do not enforce them. Consult an attorney, because some courts penalize the landlords that charge late fees which are not within the statutory limits.

Landscaping/Snow removal-This is included in all my SFH leases, but this doesn't translate well with apartments. There used to be a time when my husband would drive around in his Sedan with a lawnmower hanging out the trunk because we were responsible for cutting the grass on all of our properties. NEVER AGAIN!

Pets- I do not recommend allowing pets, but if you do permit your tenants to have a pet, then require a non-refundable pet-deposit to compensate for damage that could occur because of a pet. A pet deposit is separate from the normal security deposit, it is an additional amount. Limit the number of pets in your lease as well as the weight. Be careful with the breed of dog you allow; some insurance companies will cancel your policy if it's discovered you have a breed banned by the insurance company. Or, they may increase your premium.

Utilities- After reviewing your local and state laws regarding utilities, if possible you should require the tenant be responsible for all utilities, especially water. Typically, this only applies to SFH. Yet, this is another way of reducing expenses because when tenants are not responsible for water, they have a propensity to be very liberal with it. This can cause huge water bills, which can be a hindrance to your cash flow.

Cleaning fee- I recommend including a cleaning fee in your lease, because tenants rarely leave the place clean enough to re-rent immediately. Hiring a professional cleaning service is usually a must.

Businesses- Most leases include a clause that prohibits tenants from operating home-based businesses such as a daycare, candy store, etc. This can be a major liability for a landlord. If you discover a business is operating on your property, send the proper legal notices and pursue all courses of action to dissolve the operation. Furthermore, consider eviction.

Inspections

Inspections are really important. I always include an inspection clause in my leases, and they are quarterly. This ensures the property/unit is being properly maintained, and damages such as holes in the walls, flooring damage, or leaks are not occurring. If you neglect to do inspections twice annually at the very least, when the lease is over, you risk walking into the something that resembles the Bad Girls Club house. I had a former tenant who always made timely payments, maintained the yard, and rarely complained. Occasionally, I would ask her if there were any repairs needed; she always replied that everything was fine. She received a job offer out-of-state, and after she moved, the place was filthy; it was worse than a frat house. The tiles were drenched in dirt and mildew. Ceiling fans were saturated with dirt and dust, as was every baseboard in the house. The fridge looked like something you would see on an episode of Hoarders. The hardwood floors were scuffed and scratched and she left a roach infestation behind. I never knew she was living like a slob. She was an elementary school teacher and very pleasant to deal with. Inspect!!!

This is what happens to a new stove when you fail to inspect!

Inspections are also important to conduct for safety reasons. Checking the smoke and carbon monoxide detectors, and observing the property for any fire and safety hazards can prevent catastrophes. My experience can attest to this: I was picking up rent from a tenant, she invited me in to meet her new baby. The first thing I noticed was a large green extension cord running from the hallway into the living room. When I inquired, I learned the outlet in the laundry room wasn't functioning. Instead of notifying me, she plugged the washing machine plug into an extension cord and ran the extension cord into an outlet in an adjacent room!!! This is a major fire hazard and especially considering she had children living there.

She apologized for her negligence, citing she did not want to bother me about a small repair. I stressed to her the importance of notifying me when problems arise big or small. Sometimes tenants will try to resolve issues or make repairs they are not qualified to do. They don't want to be labeled a "problem tenant," or they may be under the impression that the fewer hassles they give the landlord, they will not face rent increases. Check on your property!!!!

Pest Control- Pest control is another expense that I have been able to shift to my SFH tenants. This is not feasible for multi-family properties. However, I always include in my lease that while they are responsible for pest control. They must use the services of my recommended pests control companies because some tenants may be tempted to hire or use a cheap unlicensed company or a relative to abate the problem.

In my experience, these cheap solutions never solve the problem, and if it's a major problem like a bed-bug infestation, it can become a very expensive problem to resolve when you want to re-rent. I had a SFH tenant who admitted she had brought back a bed-bug infestation from a short-stay at a local hospital. However, she refused to pay for re-mediation. I got stuck with the bill, and after that I included pests control as the responsibility of the tenant in my leases. Typically in multi-family properties, the landlord is responsible for all pests control; and, in Chicago, they actually have an ordinance that requires multi-family landlords to pay for exterminations else they could be fined.

Cleaning Directions- If there is anything in the property/unit that requires special cleaning, you MUST put it in writing to ensure the tenant doesn't ruin the material by using the wrong products. Things such as: granite countertops, stainless steel appliances require special cleaning products. Also, if the tub or tiles were refinished, the instructions on what products and materials to clean with should accompany the lease. I have learned in this business that the definition of clean is subjective. A cleaning guide can reinforce your standard of how the unit should be maintained. I've seen several tenants move out and leave the stove covered in grease and spills from whence they never cleaned. **IF** you have tenants that love to fry foods, stress the importance of doing a thorough kitchen cleaning after cooking. My exterminator explained that cooking grease residue is the quickest way to get a roach infestation.

Fireplace- I do not allow my tenants to operate the fireplace; it's too much of a fire hazard. However, it is a judgment call for you, if you feel your tenant is responsible enough to operate without burning down the property, by all means let have. I sleep better at night with this prohibited in my lease.

Renters Insurance- This is also required in my leases because when disasters (fires or floods) occur, my insurance will only cover the dwelling. It will not cover the tenant's belongings. This reduces the confusion that usually occurs when the tenants suffer a loss of their belongings.

Smoking- Non-smoking clauses are in most of my leases. It is accompanied by a penalty of $250 if there is smoke odor left in the unit after the tenant moves out. The only exception is if a tenant expresses and commits to staying long-term; five years or more. Then it makes financial sense because I would re-paint, re-carpet and do other small updates that would eliminate the smoking odor.

Keys- Replacement or additional set of keys are $10.

Move-in Day/ Lease Signing

Cancel the utilities-Prior to move-in day, switch the utilities out of your name. I failed to do this once, and the tenant ran up two month's worth of billing with the electric company. In my case, the tenant had a previous balance owed on her electric bill, and she couldn't transfer it to my property until it was paid but she never communicated this to me. She continued to utilize the power while I was under the impression she switched the bill. Do not entrust something this important to a tenant. In addition, NEVER agree to put the utilities in your name for a bill the tenant is responsible; you will NEVER receive payment for that bill.

Lease signing-All deposits should be paid before keys are turned over. Also, if anything occurs at lease signing or the tenant says something to give you pause, you do not have to go through with the lease. Always listen to your instinct.

Take Pictures/and Video-Conduct a complete walk-through with your camera taking pictures and video of each room in the property. This will eliminate any confusion when the tenant denies damages after the lease ends. This will also be very helpful to a judge if you ever have to go to court.

Chapter 10

TRAIN YOUR TENANT

Property Management

This brings me to the point of management. If you're a beginner and choose to self-manage, you may want to consider setting up a good cop/bad cop management style. You can have a spouse or partner act in the capacity of enforcement. Or, if you don't have those options, you can represent yourself as the property manager instead of the owner, if you struggle with being direct. At the commencement of a lease, the tenant (like an adolescent child) will test your limits. They will make big or small requests, reasonable or unreasonable to test your managerial style. Are you a push-over or a slumlord? There is a middle ground; you may want to grant a few reasonable requests but do not get into the habit of saying "yes" to every request. The tenants will take advantage of you, and this can ultimately hurt your bottom line. Stick to the lease, say more "no's" than "yeses" and keep it professional. Tenants, like children, respect and need boundaries; you have to set them. Eventually, they will respect them or at least good tenants will. There are some tenants that take pleasure in giving the landlord hell, those you should terminate as soon as possible.

I highly recommend self managing, at the beginning of your real estate career, unless it's a property out of state or the property is located several hours from where you live. It's really important to get hands-on experience when manag-ing the property. It will give you a free education on the in-tricacies of real estate and tenants. However, if you are completely opposed to self-managing in the beginning and you choose to hire a property manager, do your research. The adage "good help is hard to find" truly applies here. I have fired two property managers for lack of attentiveness, and currently seeking to hire another. Property Managers typically charge 10% of the monthly rent to manage the property, but that doesn't include any repairs. Multi-family properties are charged less based on the amount of units you have. Any repairs done, are usually charged at an hourly rate. Be sure that you place a limit on the costs of repairs that can be done without your permission.

Building a Network- This is one of the essential ingredients to building a successful real estate business. Your team should consist, of a good certified public accountant (CPA), an attorney for closings with a specialty in evictions, a very experienced contractor, a handyman for smaller repairs, a plumber, an electrician and a landscaping company for your multifamily properties. Lastly, it should include an experienced attentive property manager for when your real-estate portfolio grows so large that you can no longer self-manage. Your attorney or CPA can also help you structure your business in a more tax-friendly way. They may recommend forming a Limited Liability Company (LLC) to hold your properties for tax and liability purposes. This team will take time to build, ask other investors to share their contacts with you. This network will allow you more flexibility to travel, spend quality time with your family, or volunteer your time to whatever it is that brings you fulfillment.

Payments- There are several convenient forms in which rent payments can be received rather than physically picking up the rent. The more doors you own, the less feasible picking up rent will be. Banking applications are a popular convenient option. In addition to the several other cash apps, they have available which help make accounting simpler. Some landlords setup a checking account strictly for receiving rent payments and the tenants receive deposit slips for the account and deposit rent payments into the account. You can open a P.O. Box and have tenants mail rent payments using money order or cashier's check. NEVER have the rent payments mailed to your home. Tenants should not know where you live. It is a safety risk.

Capital Expenditures or CapEx- This is money you save each month from rent collected for expenses such as repairs, vacancy and property management. Typically this figure is 10% of the monthly rent. Example: In a rental property producing $1,000/month, you would set $100/month into a separate account. This account would finance a new roof, appliances, or the repairs needed to re-rent the unit. Always calculate CapEx into your cash flow, because in this business, things break down and you have to be prepared. Plumbing systems backup, roofs leak, parking lots need to be repaved, water heaters go out, and you know how Murphy's Law works: "anything that *can* go wrong *will* go wrong."

Security Deposits- Security deposits offer landlords some protection against tenant's destruction of the property. In my opinion, security deposits tend to elicit better behavior from tenants because tenants want the full deposit back. Seek legal advice when accepting security deposits because depending on how tenant-friendly your state is, they can have very expensive penalties if mishandled. In Chicago, lawyers are split between advising landlords on accepting security deposits or forgo the deposit to eliminate potential lawsuits from tenants.

My investment portfolio mostly consists of properties in Chicago. The Chicago rental ordinance has very punitive laws to punish landlords that mishandle security deposits. Even on a minor infraction such as not giving the tenant the 0.001% interests due on the security which ranges from 0.05 cents to $1.00 depending on the amount. In the event a landlord forgets or just failed to send the interest; the fine is double the amount of the security deposit, and you're just as well responsible for the tenant's legal fees that run thousands of dollars upward. There is no shortage of lawyers to represent these tenants. Always check the laws and ordinances where you're investing. Many landlords have exploited the move-in fee loophole to avoid the draconian ordinance. A move-in fee is a non-refundable deposit that the landlord collects prior to move-in. The fee is generally half the price or a quarter of the rent and allows the landlord to avoid adhering to the security deposit laws. However, I no longer accept move-in fees. I have reverted back to security deposits, because tenants take better care of the property when they have skin in the game. They maintain the property because they want the deposit back to carry-over to the new place.

Integrity- If you want to be in this business for the long-haul you want to demonstrate integrity. Don't make promises you can't keep. When you say something, mean what you say. Landlords already have a bad reputation; with many negative connotations associated with the profession. Make an effort to conduct your business with a high level of professionalism and remember the "golden rule." If a tenant has a valid repair, take the necessary steps to resolve the problem immediately. Don't take weeks to get back with a tenant. If the problem is taking longer than you promised to fix, communicate that to the tenant and thank them for their patience. Lack of communication is one of the main sources of tension and problems between landlords and tenants. Most importantly, refrain from writing rude or nasty texts to the tenant; keep it professional. If those texts are presented in court, it may negatively impact your case.

Buddy-buddy with the tenants. Never make the mistake of becoming too chummy with your tenants. I once had a good paying tenant. She maintained the property and was always timely with her rent payments. We became friendly with each other. We had kids around the same age, and I may have shared too much about my life. BIG MISTAKE. You can have small talk with your tenants but resist the urge to discuss your personal life. I would even warn of being too much of a listening ear to a tenants personal life because that can also hinder your business relationship with them. On the other hand, it can give you an insight into the longevity of the tenancy. Example: If the tenant complains about job stability, health or maybe the dislike for the neighborhood, you can begin to plan for a vacancy rather than a lease renewal.

Example: I had a former tenant that renewed after a one year lease. After she renewed her lease I started to notice an extra car parked in the driveway and a man was there often. She finally admitted her estranged husband had moved in with her. I felt awkward addressing the fact that she had violated her lease, by allowing an unapproved tenant to move into the house, because we had become friendly, so I let it go. Then three months later, her sickly mother moved into the property as well, another violation. This time I felt even more uncomfortable addressing this additional tenant because she informed me her mother was diagnosed with cancer.

She was still paying on time, but the service calls for repairs had increased. She inquired about moving to a bigger property to accommodate the additional tenants. I had just acquired a four-bedroom house, and we agreed to have her move in. She literally took two months to move all of her stuff from the old place to new place (insert scream and hair pulling)!!! I began to feel taken for granted and eventually things began to build up. I didn't handle the situation as professionally as I should have. Needless to say, if I had addressed the situation from the beginning, it might not have escalated to losing a tenant because that was the result.

NO fancy cars. Ok, this is an obvious one but let's just state it for the record. It is less than smart to drive a luxury car to pick-up rent or meet with your tenant, if you are representing yourself as the owner. The tenant may get the impression that you don't need the rent because you're "rich", the tenants may adopt a laid back untimely approach to paying you rent.

Pay your property taxes. The costs to redeem your taxes can be expensive, due to all the extra fees they add to the bill. Been there and got the T-shirt.

Live and Die by the lease. The lease will guide you in nearly every scenario that occurs during the tenancy. It's really important to be consistent with the lease. If the lease states a $25 late fee after five days then it's important to enforce that policy. If the tenant has a pattern of late payments and you habitually fail to charge a late fee, it may be difficult to enforce that late fee if you want to collect the late fees later. If the landlord never enforced them throughout the lease, some courts will not require that tenant to pay the late fees. Also, when you abide by the terms of the lease, you provide the tenant with consistency and its cuts down on unreasonable requests. It also garners respect from your tenants. Most problems or situations that may occur during the tenancy can be resolved by referring to the lease.

Moreover, act accordingly when there are lease violations. If the rent is past due, then you need to post a three or a five-day notice, depending upon your local state laws. The five-day notice is a demand for payment that states that, unless the rent payment is made within the time-frame of such notice, the lease will be terminated and the eviction process will commence. If the tenant moves in additional tenants, address it immediately. Don't wait for them to move in their entire extended family. Send the appropriate notices in writing and consult a real estate attorney. This maneuver follows for pets, businesses, smoking, etc. Lease violations can snow ball into other major issues, and that's why it is important to set a standard for the tenants.

Cash for Keys-Depending on the state you live in, evictions can be costly and time-consuming. The legal fees, loss of rent and the stress of dealing with a disgruntled tenant who may vandalize the property can be overwhelming. This is an understatement. In addition, even the climate you live in could cause months of delay in the eviction process, because some courts do not like to evict tenants in winter months due to the frigid temperatures, it can be dangerous and borderline deadly. Hence, cash for keys is a tool that some landlords and banks exercise when they want to eliminate the lengthy eviction process. This entails the landlord paying the tenant a lump sum of cash to vacate the property in exchange the tenant must leave in a timely fashion and leave the property in good condition. The lump sum generally ranges from $500 to $3000. It could be more or less, depending on the situation. If you ever have to utilize this method, I highly recommend consulting with an attorney to avoid any future legal issues. The agreement needs to have a release signed by the tenant, which releases you from any future lawsuits with the said tenant.

Maintaining Good Tenants

After a year lease, you should be able to determine if this a tenant you want to keep or terminate the lease, based on the tenants payment history, service calls, complaints and the upkeep the tenant has given the property. When you find the right tenant, and they have demonstrated good behavior and a good payment history, after a full lease term, you can offer one upgrade or even a small Christmas gift, i.e., gift card or fruit basket. These acts of kindness are appreciated if you have to raise the rent; it softens the blow.

Vacancy is expensive and if you can keep a GOOD tenant in the unit long-term, try to do so. If the tenant has spent a couple of years in the property, you will have to repaint and get it rent ready. If you have a good tenant that is considering moving, find out the reason, maybe you can offer a concession, if it is job-related then there may be no room for compromise.

However, if the tenant expresses concern about a rent increase, or a utility bill, you can offer a compromise that works for both parties. I recently had a similar experience with a tenant that was considering moving because of the expense of the utilities. I offered to split the water bill with her for one calendar year. It made financial sense, and it only reduced my bottom line by a small percentage. If a good tenant asks for a small upgrade, like a new toilet or new ceiling fixture, etc. you can try to oblige them, but this is only after they have completed a full year lease. Continue to offer swift service when it comes to addressing repairs or problems. Be respectful and follow through on any promises made.

Chapter 11

FOR THE LADIES

Ladies in this business, you will have a unique set of obstacles to overcome in order to succeed in this business, but it can be done. You will encounter contractors who will try to take advantage of you by inflating their prices. There may be contractors and tenants who will not take you seriously and will challenge your authority. You may find that a contractor or handyman you hired resents taking orders from women. Don't get discouraged, for there are great contractors and tenants that will respect you and your business. If you have a man in your life, a spouse/partner or your Dad, brother or cousin, ask one of these individuals to be present when you are receiving quotes for renovations. This will increase your chances of receiving a fair and reasonable quote. Also, take the time to educate yourself on the scope of the work you want to be done. Always have some level of knowledge on the steps or procedures and price of materials needed to complete the job. YouTube can be a great learning tool for construction work, and the internet can give you a ball park figure of the average costs of the job, with labor and materials. DO NOT reveal your ignorance and don't be a bimbo. So, yes ladies there is some bias towards women in the industry but nothing insurmountable. Go forward and be GREAT!!

Chapter 12

#GOALS

Set goals for the short and long term. The short-term goals could be one flip a year or one rental property per year while long-term goals can be retirement from your day job or a million dollar real estate portfolio. Real estate investing for long-term growth is a marathon, but it can be Usain Bolt-esque marathon depending on the time and money you are willing to commit and your risk propensity. Like any business, the real estate market has its ebbs and flows. Don't get discouraged when you face some challenges, persevere. You learn more from your failures than your successes. My failures are largely what inspired me to write this book. Don't limit yourself, although this book mainly focuses on SFH residential properties. Real estate is so vast: residential commercial, mobile homes, real estate development, Airbnb, retail/office commercial, storage facilities, land, cemeteries, the possibilities with real estate are endless and so is the cash flow. Find your niche and the sky is the limit.

Made in the USA
Coppell, TX
15 October 2021